D1404323

Meet the
CINCINNATI
BENGALS

BY
ZACK BURGESS

NORWOODHOUSE 🏠 PRESS

CHICAGO, ILLINOIS

NORWOOD HOUSE 🏠 PRESS

P.O. Box 316598 • Chicago, Illinois 60631
For more information about Norwood House Press please visit our website at
www.norwoodhousepress.com or call 866-565-2900.

Photo Credits:
All photos courtesy of Associated Press, except for the following: Philadelphia Chewing Gum Co. (6),
Black Book Archives (7, 15, 18), Topps, Inc. (10 both, 23), Pro Set (11 top & middle),
The Upper Deck Co. (11 bottom), NFL/Bengals (22).

Cover Photo: David Richard/Associated Press

The football memorabilia photographed for this book is part of the authors' collection. The collectibles used
for artistic background purposes in this series were manufactured by many different card companies—
including Bowman, Donruss, Fleer, Leaf, O-Pee-Chee, Pacific, Panini America, Philadelphia Chewing Gum,
Pinnacle, Pro Line, Pro Set, Score, Topps, and Upper Deck—as well as several food brands, including
Crane's, Hostess, Kellogg's, McDonald's and Post.

Designer: Ron Jaffe
Series Editors: Mike Kennedy and Mark Stewart
Project Management: Black Book Partners, LLC.
Editorial Production: Lisa Walsh

LIBRARY OF CONGRESS CATALOGING-IN-PUBLICATION DATA
Names: Burgess, Zack.
Title: Meet the Cincinnati Bengals / by Zack Burgess.
Description: Chicago, Illinois : Norwood House Press, [2016] | Series: Big
picture sports | Includes bibliographical references and index. |
Audience: Grade: K to Grade 3.
Identifiers: LCCN 2015026318| ISBN 9781599537245 (Library Edition : alk.
paper) | ISBN 9781603578271 (eBook)
Subjects: LCSH: Cincinnati Bengals (Football team)--Miscellanea--Juvenile
literature.
Classification: LCC GV956.C6 B87 2016 | DDC 796.332/640977178--dc23
LC record available at http://lccn.loc.gov/2015026318

288N—072016
Manufactured in the United States of America in North Mankato, Minnesota

CONTENTS

Words in **bold type** are defined on page 24.

The Bengals celebrate a touchdown.

CALL ME A BENGAL

The Bengal tiger is one of the smartest and most powerful animals on earth. The Cincinnati Bengals are smart and powerful, too. They look for athletes with special talents. Even so, every player knows that his skills must fit into a bigger picture for the team to win.

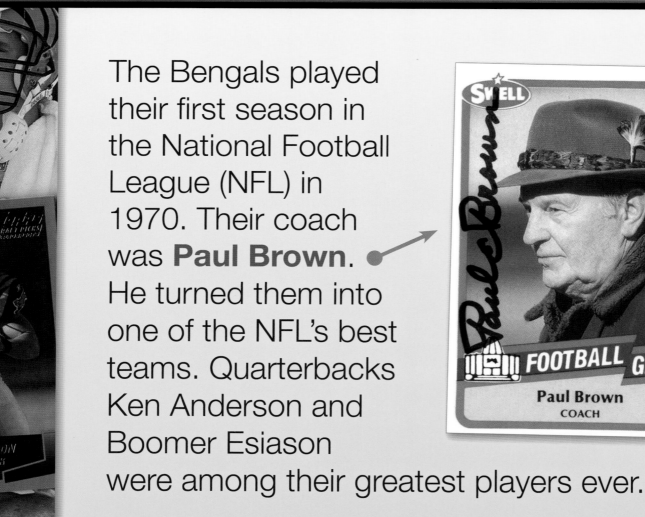

The Bengals played their first season in the National Football League (NFL) in 1970. Their coach was **Paul Brown**. He turned them into one of the NFL's best teams. Quarterbacks Ken Anderson and Boomer Esiason were among their greatest players ever.

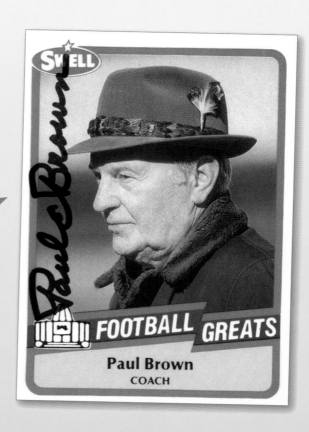

SWELL

FOOTBALL GREATS

Paul Brown
COACH

Boomer Esiason looks for an open receiver.

The Cincinnati skyline rises above Paul Brown Stadium.

Best Seat in the House

The Bengals play in Paul Brown Stadium. It was named in memory of their first coach. Fans call the stadium "The Jungle." It can be a scary place to play. Every seat has a good view of the field. And almost everyone can see the Cincinnati skyline.

Shoe Box

The trading cards on these pages show some of the best Bengals ever.

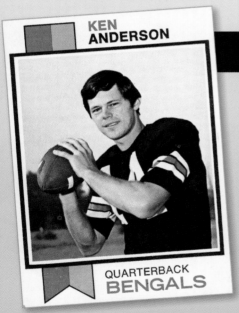

Ken Anderson

Quarterback · 1971–1986

Ken almost never threw a bad pass. He was voted **All-Pro** and the NFL's Most Valuable Player (MVP) in 1981.

Isaac Curtis

Wide Receiver · 1973–1984

Isaac was a track star in college. He had 53 touchdown catches for the Bengals.

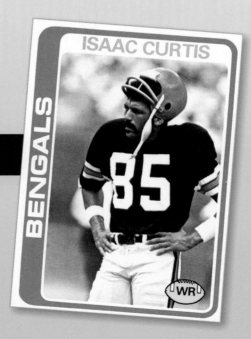

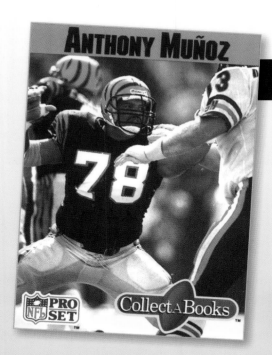

ANTHONY MUNOZ

TACKLE · 1980-1992

Anthony was the best offensive lineman of his time. He was voted into the **Hall of Fame** in 1998.

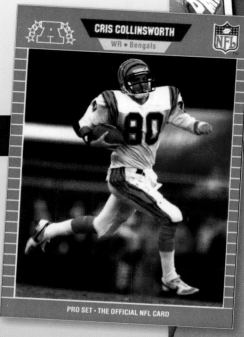

CRIS COLLINSWORTH

WIDE RECEIVER · 1981-1988

Cris was tall and had good speed. He was great at finding holes in the defense.

A.J. GREEN

WIDE RECEIVER · FIRST YEAR WITH TEAM: 2011

A.J. continued the team tradition of great pass-catchers. He made the **Pro Bowl** in each of his first five seasons.

THE BIG PICTURE

Look at the two photos on page 13. Both appear to be the same. But they are not. There are three differences. Can you spot them?

Answers on page 23.

13

TRUE OR FALSE?

Chad Johnson was a star receiver. Two of these facts about him are **TRUE**. One is **FALSE**. Do you know which is which?

1 Chad caught more than 80 passes five years in a row for the Bengals.

2 Chad loved tigers so much that he once bought five Bengal cubs.

3 For five years, Chad changed his last name to Ochocinco, which is Spanish for "8–5."

Answer on page 23.

Chad Johnson heads for the end zone.

Who Dey
high-fives a
young fan.

Go Bengals, Go!

Bengals fans have a special chant during games. It goes, "Who dey, who dey, who dey think gonna beat them Bengals? Nobody!" The chant started when the team was on its way to the Super Bowl in 1981. Who Dey is now the name of the team's mascot!

ON THE MAP

Here is a look at where five Bengals were born, along with a fun fact about each.

 CARSON PALMER • FRESNO, CALIFORNIA
Carson led the NFL with 32 touchdown passes in 2005.

 ANDY DALTON • KATY, TEXAS
Andy threw for more than 3,000 yards in each of his first five seasons.

 KEN RILEY • BARTOW, FLORIDA
Ken had 65 **interceptions** for the Bengals.

 BOOMER ESIASON • WEST ISLIP, NEW YORK
Boomer played in the Pro Bowl three times for the Bengals.

 HORST MUHLMANN • DORTMUND, GERMANY
Horst was a soccer goalkeeper before he joined the Bengals as a kicker.

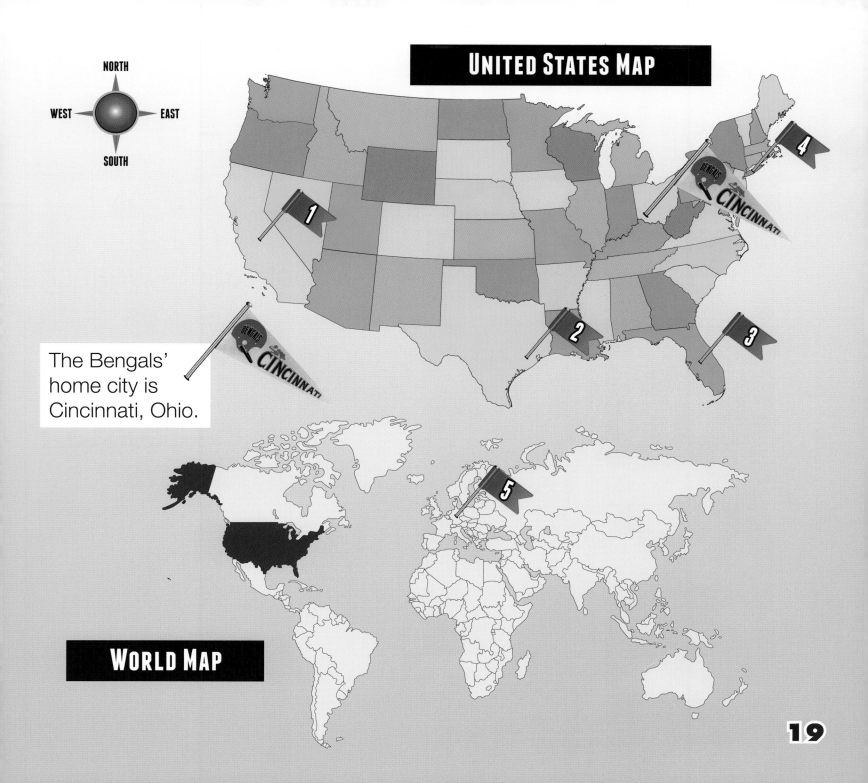

UNITED STATES MAP

NORTH
WEST EAST
SOUTH

The Bengals' home city is Cincinnati, Ohio.

WORLD MAP

HOME AND AWAY

Football teams wear different uniforms for home and away games. The main colors of the Bengals are orange, black, and white. They use a stripe design to remind fans of a tiger.

Rey Maualuga wears the Bengals' home uniform.

The Bengals' helmet also has orange and black stripes. They have used this design since 1981. It is one of the NFL's coolest helmets.

WE WON!

The Bengals reached the Super Bowl for the first time after the 1981 season. Quarterback Ken Anderson and running back **Pete Johnson** led the way. The Bengals returned to the big game after the 1988 season. Boomer Esiason was named the league MVP that year.

RECORD BOOK

These Bengals set team records.

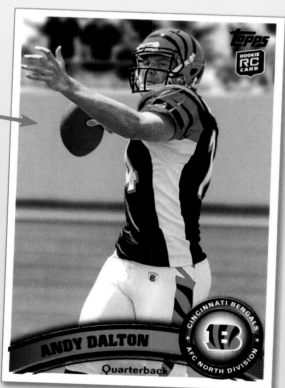

TOUCHDOWN PASSES		RECORD
Season: **Andy Dalton** (2013)		33
Career: Ken Anderson		197

TOUCHDOWN CATCHES		RECORD
Season: Carl Pickens (1995)		17
Career: Chad Johnson		66

RUSHING TOUCHDOWNS		RECORD
Season: Ickey Woods (1988)		15
Career: Pete Johnson		64

ANSWERS FOR THE BIG PICTURE
#94 changed to #49, the 3 on #53 is backward, and the orange pylon on the field has disappeared.

ANSWER FOR TRUE AND FALSE
#2 is false. Chad never bought five Bengal cubs.

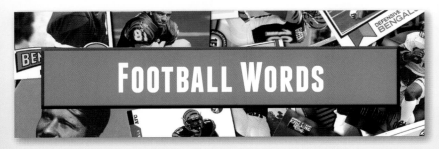
Football Words

All-Pro
An honor given to the best NFL player at each position.

Hall of Fame
The museum in Canton, Ohio, where football's greatest players are honored.

Interceptions
Passes caught by a defensive player.

Pro Bowl
The NFL's annual all-star game.

Index

Photos are on **BOLD** numbered pages.

About the Author

Zack Burgess has been writing about sports for more than 20 years. He has lived all over the country and interviewed lots of All-Pro football players, including Brett Favre, Eddie George, Jerome Bettis, Shannon Sharpe, and Rich Gannon. Zack was the first African American beat writer to cover Major League Baseball when he worked for the *Kansas City Star*.

About the Bengals

Learn more at these websites:
www.bengals.com • www.profootballhof.com
www.teamspiritextras.com/Overtime/html/bengals.html